# RELIGIONS OF THE WORLD™

# I Am Buddhist

❊ DANIEL P. QUINN ❊

The Rosen Publishing Group's
## PowerKids Press™
New York

Published in 1996, 2003 by The Rosen Publishing Group, Inc.
29 East 21st Street, New York, NY 10010

**Revised Edition 2003**

Editor: Gillian Houghton
Book Design: Erin McKenna and Kim Sonsky
Text Revisions: Jennifer Way

Photo credits: Cover © Christophe Loviny/CORBIS; p. 4 © Steve Satushek/Image Bank; pp. 7, 20 © Jack Kurtz/Impact Visuals; p. 8 © Scott Thode/International Stock; p. 11 © Patrick Ramsey/International Stock; p. 12 © Orion/International Stock; p. 15 © Hoa-Qui/Liaison International; p. 16 © Rod Low; p. 19 © Ira Lipsky/International Stock.

Quinn, Daniel P.
   I am Buddhist / Daniel P. Quinn
      p.   cm. — (Religions of the world)
   Includes index.
   Summary: A young Chinese girl living in San Francisco with her family describes the principles and ceremonies of Buddhism.
   ISBN 0-8239-6814-6
   1. Buddhism—Juvenile literature. [1. Buddhism.] I. Series: Religions of the world (Rosen Publishing Group)
BQ4032.Q5 1996
294.3—dc20                                        96-6978

Manufactured in the United States of America

# Contents

# Being Buddhist

My name is Yuyen. I live in San Francisco, California. I am Chinese and am a Buddhist. There are many kinds of Buddhism, but all Buddhists are followers of the Buddha, or "the **enlightened** one." The Buddha was a monk who lived in India about 2,500 years ago. Through **meditation**, he came to understand how to be free from suffering. He traveled, teaching others how to reach enlightenment. Buddhists try to become enlightened by following his teachings.

◀ From the time that they are children, Buddhists follow the Buddha's teachings.

# In the Temple

A Buddhist temple houses many objects that remind us of the Buddha's teachings. In the main room, called the shrine, there is an altar, or table, and a large statue of the Buddha. There are many kinds of Buddha statues used to represent the many qualities of the Buddha. One statue shows the Buddha's hand resting in his lap. This statue represents finding peace with oneself. One statue shows his right hand touching the ground, showing his determination. People bring offerings of flowers, food, water, and **incense** to the altar.

People make offerings at the altar out of respect for the Buddha's wisdom. ▶

# Refuge in the Buddha

We learn to take **refuge** in the examples that the Buddha set during his life, in the things he said, and in the things he did. "Taking refuge" means receiving protection, comfort, and care. In Buddhism, one can take refuge in the Buddha, his teachings, and the community of people whom we encounter on our path to enlightenment. Understanding that the Buddha was a real person reminds us that we can become enlightened, too. Taking refuge in the Buddha is the first of what are known as the Three Jewels of Buddhism.

◄ Buddhists carry out the teachings of the
Buddha in part by caring for others.

# Refuge in the Dharma

The second jewel of Buddhism is taking refuge in the **dharma**. The dharma are the teachings of the Buddha. Dharma also means duty, goodness, truth, and the nature of the self. This means that we take refuge in the Buddha's teachings as well as in the examples that he set during his life. We learn to care for others, to do good things, to follow rules, and to be honest. Taking refuge in the dharma helps one on the path to enlightenment.

A Buddhist might spend time with an elderly neighbor, to care for another person according to the teachings of the Buddha. ▶

# Refuge in the Sangha

The third jewel of Buddhism is taking refuge in the sangha. The sangha is our commitment to leading a moral life, or good life, both in our personal life and in our community. This community includes all people who try to live a good life, all animals, and all of nature. In order to show this commitment to the community, we follow rules. One of these rules is that we should not destroy life. For this reason, many Buddhists are **vegetarians**, which means they do not eat meat.

◀ Buddhists learn that all living things should be given respect.

# Karma

Buddhists believe in **karma**. Karma means that every action has an effect. The law of karma says that a person's actions are revisited upon them. If I do something kind, something good will happen to me. If I do something unkind, something bad will come back to me. My mother says that we should always try to be kind.

This young girl is a Buddhist from Thailand. ▶

# Bodhisattva

Guan Yin is a very important **bodhisattva**. A bodhisattva is an enlightened being on the path to **nirvana** who chooses to help others achieve enlightenment. Guan Yin also protects people from dangers such as fire and sickness. We have a statue of Guan Yin in our house. My family honors her and prays to her every morning.

◀ Guan Yin is important to many Buddhists in China and Japan. This statue of Guan Yin is in Japan.

# Buddha Day

Buddha Day is a special day for us. It is celebrated on the day of the first full moon in the month of May. It was on this day that the Buddha was born, reached enlightenment, died, and reached nirvana. My family puts a statue of the baby Buddha in a bowl. We put flowers over the statue. We pour perfumed water or tea over the baby Buddha. This ceremony represents the cleansing of our thoughts and actions. The temple is brightly decorated with flowers and banners. The altar is crowded with offerings. It is a happy time.

There are statues of the Buddha throughout the world. This statue is in Taiwan. ▶

# Honoring the Ancestors

My father and mother have taught me that an important part of Chinese Buddhism is honoring one's **ancestors**. Ancestors are the relatives who have lived before us, such as our grandparents and great-grandparents. On special days, we light incense in front of a picture of my grandparents. We leave offerings of rice cakes in front of the picture. We also sing special songs and pray.

◀ One way in which Buddhists honor their ancestors is by lighting prayer sticks.

# The Sutras

There are many stories about the Buddha and his life. The Buddha's first followers remembered and repeated the Buddha's stories and lessons. These stories have been recorded in books called **sutras**. The stories tell us about what the Buddha taught and how he lived. They tell the story of how he came to understand the meaning of life. We use parts of the sutras as prayers. We also learn from them. The sutras were originally written on the leaves of palm trees in Pali and Sanskrit, two ancient Indian languages.

# Glossary

**ancestors** (AN-ses-terz) Relatives who lived long ago.

**bodhisattva** (boh-dee-SAHT-vuh) A pure being who helps others reach enlightenment.

**dharma** (DAR-muh) Teachings of the Buddha.

**enlightened** (en-LY-tend) Having great understanding.

**incense** (IN-sents) Spice or scent that is burned.

**karma** (KAR-muh) The force of a person's actions, which shows that every action has an effect.

**meditation** (meh-dih-TAY-shun) The act of keeping one's thoughts on something.

**nirvana** (ner-VAH-nuh) The final stage of enlightenment in Buddhism.

**refuge** (REH-fyooj) Shelter, comfort, safety.

**sutras** (SOO-truz) Books about the Buddha and his life.

**vegetarians** (veh-juh-TER-ee-unz) People who do not eat meat.

23

# Index

# Web Sites

Due to the changing nature of Internet links, PowerKids Press has developed an online list of Web sites related to the subject of this book. This site is updated regularly. Please use this link to access the list:
www.powerkidslinks.com/rotw/buddhi/